AF557848

Belt and Road Initiative Grand Strategy

Challenges Gallore

Belt and Road Initiative Grand Strategy

Challenges Gallore

Dipanjan Roy Chaudhury

HAR-ANAND
PUBLICATIONS PVT LTD

HAR-ANAND PUBLICATIONS PVT LTD
E-49/3, Okhla Industrial Area, Phase-II, New Delhi-110020
Tel.: 41603490
E-mail: info@haranandbooks.com/haranand@rediffmail.com
Shop online at: www.haranandbooks.com

Published by Ashok Gosain and Ashish Gosain for
Har-Anand Publications Pvt Ltd

Printed in India at Aakash Press.

Contents

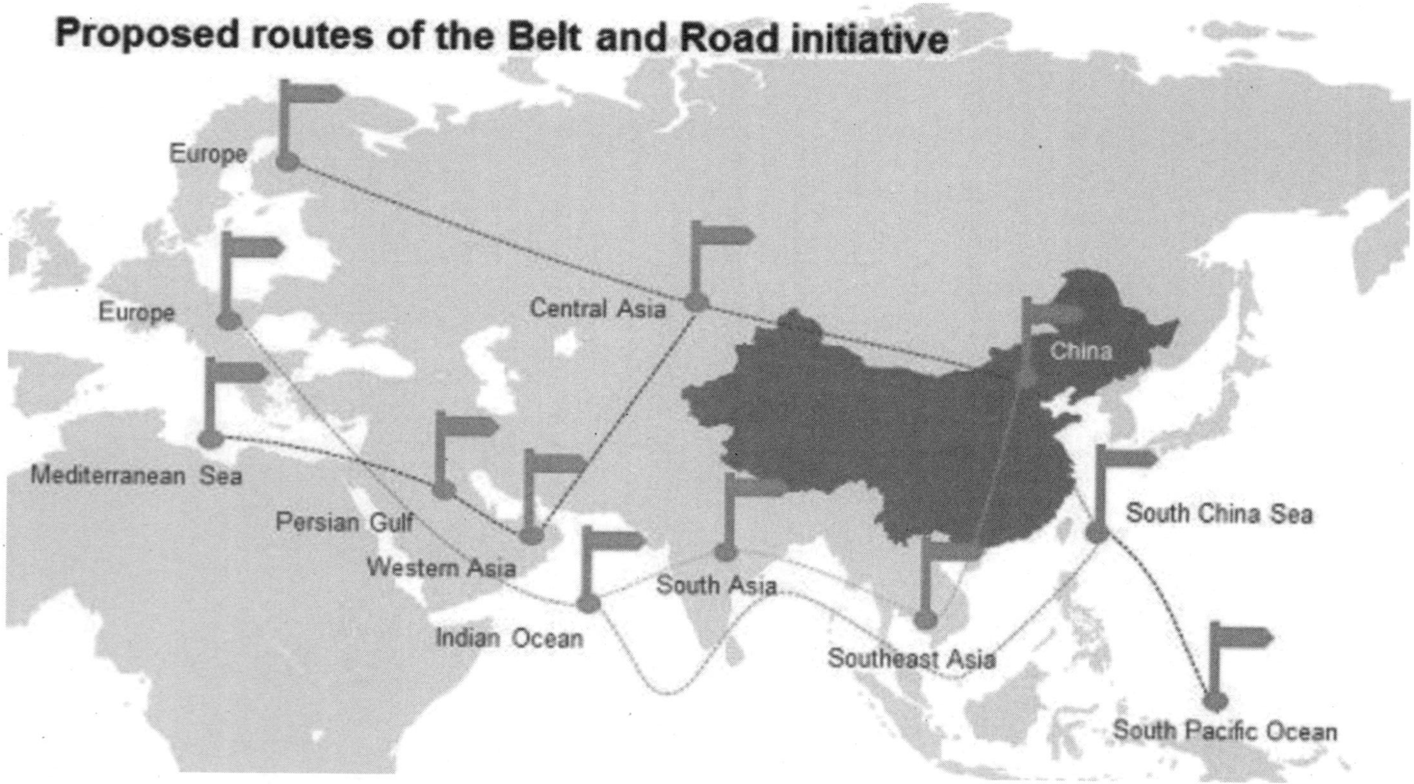

Proposed BRI Route. *Source:* Voices on Central Asia.

Introduction

The One Belt One Road (OBOR) which later has been as the Belt and Road Initiative (BRI) has been a transformative concept in the contemporary geo-politics. While BRI supporters would describe the concept as nothing new as it brought together several Chinese funded projects across continents under one umbrella, the initiative in real terms is a tool to expand Chinese influence globally. It is a signature instrument of President Xi Jinping who has been at the helm of affairs when People's Republic of China completed 70 years of existence.

BRI is a strategy which President Xi feel would put him at par with his predecessors Mao and Deng and ensure his place in geo-politics. However, the very nature of BRI which China's neighbour India continues to oppose on the grounds of violation of sovereignty and lack of transparency, has drawn more criticism than kudos. While Italy a G-7 nation decided to join BRI, criticism of BRI as an instrument that is pushing countries into debt trap and China's orbit of influence has been far and wide.

As a correspondent who focusses on foreign affairs for *The Economic Times,* India's no. 1 *Financial Daily,* I have been focussing on articles highlighting various elements of BRI. Many of these articles have been quoted by think-tanks and universities world over. As the second BRI Summit is on the anvil I felt it necessary to bring out a selection of my articles on BRI published in *The Economic Times* over the past two years in the form of monograph. Hope the readers will find this useful.

I am grateful to *The Economic Times* editors Bodhisatva Ganguly, Saubhik Chakraborty, Javed Sayed and Pranab Dhal Samanta for giving me opportunity to pen the articles on BRI since 2017. I am also grateful to my spouse Aparajita Gupta for bearing with me while I focused on research on BRI while writing the articles in *The Economic Times.*

April 2019
New Delhi

Dipanjan Roy Chaudhury

PLA troops to protect BRI. *Source:* National Security College, ANU.

Iron Brother. *Source:* The Weekly Pakistan.

Villages near Gwadar Port reels under water shortage. *Source:* Wikimedia.

I

CPEC: Changing Equations in South Asia

China, Pakistan Expand Business at Economic Corridor

New Delhi: Pakistan and China have decided to widen the scope of the China Pakistan Economic Corridor (CPEC) including expansion of activities in the Gwadar Port. The development could mean a headache for India which already has concerns regarding the CPEC as it overlaps with Pakistan-occupied Kashmir.

The CPEC is China's flagship project under its belt and road initiative, which aims to link China with economies in southeast and central Asia.

People familiar with the CPEC plan told ET that China recently signed new agreements with Pakistan to launch industrial, agriculture and socio-economic projects under this initiative. The corridor also plans to promote the petrochemical, hydrocarbon, as well as maritime sectors through Gwadar Port, they said.

The decisions were taken at a recent meeting of the CPEC's Joint Cooperation Committee (JCC) in Beijing. The industrial cooperation with China would help relocate industry and operationalisation of four special economic zones (SEZs) in

Rashakai, Dhabeji, Faisalabad and Islamabad in Pakistan, the country's Planning, Development and Reforms Minister, Khusro Baktiar, told reporters in Lahore on Sunday.

China has reportedly agreed to give a grant of $1 billion for development of education, health, irrigation and less-developed areas of Pakistan. Islamabad had also urged Beijing to set up light engineering and manufacturing units in the country to boost the local economy, which is facing a crisis due to foreign exchange shortage.

The Imran Khan-led government is understood to have prepared a master plan for the Gwadar Port, which has been built with Chinese assistance, and could also work as a naval base for China. China is in the process of creating a colony only for Chinese nationals at Gwadar. Pakistan wants to develop hydrocarbon and petrochemical complexes in Gwadar, besides boosting the fisheries sector through the port.

However, India-backed Chabahar Port in Iran, which is close to Gwadar, has the potential to rival Gwadar. The Chabahar Port is functional and being used for transporting goods to Afghanistan. Also, an international conference in Chabahar city next month would help in drawing a roadmap for Eurasian countries to have footprints in Chabahar.

Besides, Pakistan wants to promote the agriculture sector under CPEC by inviting Chinese companies to explore investment opportunities and leverage agro value chains. Khan, in a recent internal meeting, is understood to have made it clear that early completion of CPEC projects was in Pakistan's interest and stressed that he wants to follow the Chinese model for poverty alleviation.

The Economic Times, New Delhi 22 January 2019

As Part of CPEC, 'Chinese Only' Colony Coming up in Pakistan

China is building a city for 5,00,000 Chinese nationals at a cost of $150 million in Gwadar as part of China-Pakistan Economic Corridor (CPEC). This will be the first such Chinese city in South Asia.

Half-a-million Chinese citizens, who will be housed in this proposed city by 2022, will be workforce for the financial district that Beijing is planning to set up in the Pakistani port city of Gwadar. Only Chinese citizens will live in this gated zone, which basically means that Pakistan will be used as a colony of China.

ET has learnt that the China-Pak Investment Corporation bought the 3.6-million square foot International Port City and will build a $150-million gated community for the anticipated 5,00,000 Chinese professionals who will be located by 2022 and work in its proposed new financial district in Gwadar.

China has such complexes or subcity for its nationals who are part of the workforce for projects in Africa and Central Asia. There are allegations that Chinese have also moved to acquire territory in eastern Russia and northern part of Myanmar, and such exclusive zones for Chinese citizens are also giving rise to considerable local resentment

Beijing has invested in Pakistan's pipelines, railways, highways, power plants, industrial areas and mobile networks to advance the geographical mid-way link for BRI.

In return, Chinese inland manufacturing cities have secured better links to shipping lanes and newly made free trade zones through railways, port renovation and blockchain technology.

Of the 39 proposed CPEC projects, 19 are either already completed or underway, with China spending over $18.5 billion since 2015.

The Economic Times, New Delhi, 21 August 2018

CHINA WORRIED BAN ON AZHAR WILL MAKE JAISH TARGET CPEC

China, which has to take a call within the next week to change its stand on proscribing Masood Azhar, is now said to be worried that such an action will make the China-Pakistan Economic Corridor (CPEC) that passes through Pakistan-Occupied Kashmir (POK) a target of the Jaish-e-Mohammad (JeM).

ET has reliably gathered that China, which is believed to be actively considering this time to support the fresh move against Azhar in the UN Security Council (UNSC), is also looking at tying down Pakistan with security guarantees.

The CPEC passes through not only POK and Gilgit-Baltistan, but also the Mansehra district in Khyber Pakhtunkhwa where Balakot is located. Most terror training camps are located in this district as it abuts POK. The Indian Air Force had struck one of the largest JeM camps in Balakot after the Pulwama attack.

China has recently acquired large tracts of land near Balakot for the CPEC. Significantly, the Karakoram Highway that links Pakistan with China through POK also passes through Mansehra.

Chinese vice foreign minister Kong Xuanyou visited Pakistan on March 5-6 in this backdrop. He is believed to have discussed guarantees for CPEC, which is Beijing's flagship project under the mega Belt and Road Initiative (BRI). The second BRI summit is due early April, according to reliable sources. Around 10,000 Chinese nationals are working on various CPEC-related projects.

India, for its part, is being very cautious as China weighs options ahead of the March13 deadline at the UNSC. The proposal on designating Azhar as a global terrorist under UNSC 1267 resolution was initiated by France and backed by other three permanent members—the United States, United Kingdom and Russia.

Proposals Blocked Thrice

China has thrice blocked proposals to list Azhar but is now engaged in intense internal consultations on the UNSC proposal given that it comes right after a major terror attack in India.

From New Delhi's standpoint, Beijing is the only road-block to proscribing Azhar.

The UNSC chair, which is currently Indonesia, has notified that unless it hears to the contrary by Wednesday, 13 March 2019, 3:00 p.m., the Security Council will take it that the members of the Sanctions Committee have no objection to Azhar's addition to the 1267 ISIL (Da'esh) and Al-Qaida Sanctions List.

CPEC is called the jewel in the crown of China and Pakistan's 'all-weather friendship'. The corridor links China to the Arabian Sea and beyond through the Gwadar port.

Many associated power projects and ancillary infrastructure are being built under the CPEC.

Besides this, China sent a team of socio-economic development experts to Pakistan last week to firm up projects in six newly identified areas of health, education, water supply, vocational training, poverty alleviation and agriculture.

China also views Pakistan as a gateway to reach out to the Islamic world as it gets increasingly concerned by radicalisation among the Uyghurs under the East Turkestan Independence Movement (ETIM). It's said ETIM has developed links with Pakistan-based terror groups like the Lashkar-e-Taiba.

India has always felt that Pakistan military's control over these groups has worked in ensuring that Chinese interests are protected. However, terror attacks in Balochistan and Sindh against Chinese personnel and workers have increased, forcing Beijing to revisit these old assumptions.

The Economic Times, New Delhi, 8 March 2019

CPEC COULD DESTROY PAKISTAN ECONOMY AND SOCIETY

The China-Pakistan-Economic-Corridor (CPEC)—flagship project under the mega One Belt One Road (OBOR) initiative—is not merely a corridor that Pakistan is hoping will transform its economy but rather a project that may wreck its finances and societal structure.

A 15-year master plan of CPEC that has come to light reveals that Pakistan will be fully subjugated by China under the current terms and conditions of the project.

The master plan, a copy of which is seen by ET, envisages a deep and broad-based penetration of most sectors of Pakistan's economy as well as its society by Chinese enterprises and culture. The plan spells out in detail what Chinese intentions and priorities are in Pakistan for the next 15 years. It may be recalled that China has decided to invest $62 billion for the CPEC project.

Under the plan, thousands of acres of agricultural land will be leased out to Chinese enterprises in Pakistan to set up "demonstration projects" in areas ranging from seed varieties to irrigation technology.

A system of monitoring and surveillance will be built in cities from Peshawar to Karachi with 24-hour video recording on roads and busy marketplaces for law and order.

Besides, as the per master plan, a national fibre-optic backbone will be built for Pakistan not only for internet traffic, but also terrestrial distribution of broadcast TV, which will cooperate with Chinese media in the "dissemination of Chinese culture." A similar Sinification is visible in the Mandalay town of Myanmar which has impacted local architecture and culture. It remains to be seen how a conservative section of the Pakistani society reacts to the influence of Chinese culture.

In some areas, the plan is to build on a market presence already established by Chinese enterprises—for instance, Haier in household appliances, China Mobile and Huawei in telecommunications, and China Metallurgical Group Corporation in mining and minerals.

A key thrust of the plan lies in agriculture. Pakistan will also become a market for agricultural produce from Western China and this will adversely impact local producers, alleged Pakistani civil society activists. From provision of seeds and other inputs, such as fertiliser, credit and pesticides, Chinese enterprises will also operate their own farms, processing facilities for fruits and vegetables and grain. Logistics companies will operate a large storage and transportation system for agrarian produce, as per the CPEC master plan. Chinese enterprises will take the lead in each field.

Experts on Chinese economy claim that Beijing's goal through CPEC is to improve the agriculture sector of certain western provinces. The plan proposes to harness the work of the Xinjiang Production and Construction Corps to bring mechanization as well as scientific technique in livestock breeding, development of hybrid varieties and precision irrigation to Pakistan. It sees its main opportunity as helping the Kashgar Prefecture, a territory within the larger Xinjiang Autonomous Zone, which is poverty ridden.

FIBRE OPTIC WORRIES

One of the oldest priorities for the Chinese government since talks on CPEC began is fibre optic connectivity between China and Pakistan. An MoU for such a link was signed in July 2013 which may impact India's security. "Moreover, China's telecom services to Africa need to be transferred in Europe, so there's a certain hidden danger of the overall security," says the plan.

The plan also envisages a terrestrial cable across the Khunjerab pass to Islamabad, and a submarine landing station of cable in Gwadar. Gwadar, as per the plan, "is positioned as the direct hinterland connecting Balochistan and Afghanistan."

The expanded bandwidth will enable terrestrial broadcast of digital HD television, called Digital Television Terrestrial Multimedia Broadcasting (DTMB). This is envisioned as more than just a technological contribution. According to the master plan, "It is a cultural transmission carrier. The future cooperation between Chinese and Pakistani media will be beneficial to disseminating Chinese culture in Pakistan, further enhancing mutual understanding between the two peoples and the traditional friendship between the two countries."

"There is a plan to build a pilot safe city in Peshawar, which faces a fairly severe security situation in northwestern

Pakistan," the plan says, following which the initiative will be extended to major cities such as Islamabad, Lahore and Karachi. This may see deployment of Chinese forces in Pakistan with a direct bearing on Indian security.

Importantly, Pakistan's federal and involved local governments should also bear part of the responsibility for financing through issuing sovereign guarantee, according to the plan.

The Economic Times, New Delhi, 18 May 2017

II

BRI: China's Geo-Political Tool Confront Challenges

China Admits Challenges in BRI Amid Pushback

China has admitted that it may have to make some adjustments to Belt and Road-related works, an acknowledgement of concerns that the mega projects it is implementing in India's neighbourhood risk pushing countries to debt trap or fail to meet their needs.

Wang Jun, deputy director of the Department of Information at the China Centre for International Economic Exchanges, told the Global Times that it was "normal and understandable that development focus can change at different stages in different countries, especially with changes in government. So, China can also make some strategic adjustments when cooperating with these countries."

These remarks came in the backdrop of opposition within the Pak government on the financing of the China–Pakistan Economic Corridor, and pushback by Myanmar and Malaysia. The Chinese concession also comes amid increased international attention on China's crackdown on Muslims in Xinjiang.

Beijing's closest ally, Pakistan, sprung a surprise when it demanded visiting Chinese foreign minister Wang Yi to expand

Protests against BRI in Australia. *Source:* The Epoch Times.

Backlash against Chinese projects. *Source:* The ASEAN Post.

Protest against China in Central Asia. *Source:* Modern Diplomacy.

Beijing's $60-billion-plus investment in the corridor, the flagship project under the Belt and Road initiative, to include manufacturing and poverty-reduction programmes.

Besides, Pakistan is seeking an IMF bailout package and it would require Islamabad to provide chapter and verse of the finances of Belt-and-Road-related projects. These have so far been kept under wrap.

More recently, protests against forced resettlement of eight Nepali villages have influenced CWE Investment Corporation, a subsidiary of China Three Gorges, to consider pulling out of a 750-mw hydropower project. CWE said it was looking at cancelling the project.

Malaysian Prime Minister Mahathir Mohamad has suspended or cancelled $26 billion in Chinese-funded projects since his election victory in May. According to Malaysia's Chinese-language Seehua news site China Petroleum Pipeline Engineering Company officially announced that it received notification from the Malaysia government that three Chinese oil and gas pipeline projects (MPP, TSGP and Petronas) have been formally closed. These three projects all completed only less than 15% of the work but most of the payments had been made to China.

Myanmar is negotiating a significant scaling back of a Chinese-funded port project on the Bay of Bengal—from one that was proposed to cost $7.3 billion to a more modest development that would cost $1.3 billion—in a bid to avoid shouldering unsustainable debt.

China has written off an undisclosed amount of Tajik debt in exchange for ceding control of around 1,158 square kilometres of disputed territory close to the Central Asian nation's border with Xinjiang.

Meanwhile, Zambia, following in the footsteps of Sri Lanka that was forced to give China a major stake in its port of Hambantota because it could not service its debt, saw itself this month left with no choice but to hand over control of its international airport as well as a state power company to China.

The Economic Times, New Delhi, 24 September 2018

CHINA'S BRI COMES UNDER SEVERE CRITICISM ON ITS FIFTH ANNIVERSARY

Future of China's Belt and Road Initiative looks bleak with countries across continents getting into debt trap and internal troubles rising, according to a Chinese affairs expert.

Chinese affairs expert Qian Benli, in an article published at the Committee for the Abolition of Illegitimate Debt (CADTM), an international network of individuals and local committees from across Europe and Latin America, Africa and Asia, has cited various news reports to ascertain the adverse effects of OBOR, both on the domestic and international fronts.

In August 2018, Malaysian Prime Minister Mahathir Mohamad cancelled the East Coast Rail Link (ECRL) and the Trans-Sabah Gas Pipeline (TSGP) projects, which were part of China's OBOR initiative, saying his country's top priority was to minimize its debt and loans.

Earlier an article in the Financial Times in July 2018 pointed out that 234 out of 1,674 Chinese-invested infrastructure projects announced in 66 Belt and Road countries since 2013 have encountered difficulties.

Alluding to a report by Hong Kong-based website, Borderless Movement, Qian claims OBOR has created negative effects in foreign countries, and led to neglect of China's domestic consequences including corruption, financial deficiency, the rise of xenophobia, among others.

"It seems as though the ordinary people of China generally do not benefit from the expansionist strategy of the state; moreover, some of them are also the victims of the Chinese ruling class' global ambition," writes Qian in his detailed report.

China is taking over Zambia's international airport after a debt instalment default, while Congo is in deep debt due to China-funded projects.

"Before becoming General Secretary in November 2012, Xi was quite a mediocre figure in the party, and this probably was one of the reasons that induced the party elders to pick him. Thus Xi and his followers needed sound political and economic accomplishments to consolidate their power. Packaging all the existing overseas projects into a shiny new box under Xi's name was a quick way to gain credit," the article by Qian claims.

It cites the website run by the Supreme People's Procuratorate of China to ascertain its findings which claim that corruption occurs in the processes of decision making, examination and approval, land acquisition, and material procurement of the OBOR projects.

Citing chinanews.com, the article claims the fact that 'due to the untransparent nature of China's anti-corruption campaign and the authority's efforts to protect the image of OBOR, it is very hard to acquire the details of OBOR-related corruption or prove rumors. However, 170 senior executives of China's state-owned enterprises (SOEs) have been prosecuted by the authorities since 2013 and many of these SOEs have been involved in OBOR projects.'

"After terms are reached with a host country, funds are transferred directly into the Beijing-based bank accounts of China's state-owned enterprises, which build the project often with Chinese materials. This is a model Beijing has employed extensively in Africa," claims the author in the piece.

Quoting an article published by Foreign Policy, it brings forward the fact that although most of the cash will never leave China, the sheer quantity of equipment and materials, such as steel, concrete, and timber, needed to produce so many projects will provide ample opportunity for pilferage and other types of on-site malfeasance.

"Even if individual corruption is not considered, so far OBOR is making the state lose money rather than bringing back profits. Some political dissidents also argue that members of the Chinese ruling class are using OBOR as a mean of money laundering or even to secretly transfer national wealth overseas in preparation for their lives after the collapse of the CPC regime," claims the author.

Further drawing a comparison between Military build-up and "Wolf Warriors," the author outlines the details of project claiming that the mega construction and infrastructure projects China invests in overseas require the Chinese state to make considerable efforts to protect its assets and personnel from various direct threats such as pirates, local warlords and China's rivals.

"If Beijing continues the expansionist strategy, it would have to spend more on the military build-up to protect its overseas interests However, in the current economic situation, further increasing military spending means cuts to education, social welfare or other public spending," the write-up reads.

Citing a report by Xinhua, it highlights that 'the rise of xenophobia reflects this dilemma faced by the party. In order to achieve the soft power building goal of OBOR, China now hosts a large number of international students from OBOR countries- in 2017, they numbered 317.2 thousand, or 64.85% of the overall international students in China. They enjoy much better government benefits than China's domestic students, such as higher scholarships.'

It further quotes a report from toutiaosg.com, to give an instance of the fact that a lot of online speeches blame international students from Africa for having caused a large increase in AIDS cases in China.

Terming it a 'Purge Instead of Prosperity,' the report further summarises the statistics by China Daily and Singapore-based Channel *NewsAsia* to establish that "the frontier and hub of the Silk Road Economic Belt (One Belt), which Beijing has promised to bring prosperity and stability to Xinjiang Uyghur Autonomous Region (XUAR). In some ways, this is being achieved. XUAR's average annual GDP growth from 2012 to 2016 was 9.3 percent, higher than the national level. In 2017, investment in fixed assets in XUAR was the highest in China and more than 50,000 companies had been established or had branches set up there."

Qian also cites a report by The Diplomat and claims that the incidents of violence and terrorism have increased in XUAR in recent years, but they are largely caused by the displacement of Muslim communities and the 'aggressive attempts to assimilate Uyghurs into Han culture through targeted educational and work programs that incentivise the learning of Mandarin and integration into the Chinese state's vision of modernization.'

Recalling that this year marks the fifth anniversary of OBOR initiative, Benli also highlights the lack of benefit to the Chinese people through this project and writes, "They hardly ever mention any benefit brought back to the Chinese people. No figure about any relevant increases in terms of jobs, foreign exchange reserves or domestic living standards has been found."

The Economic Times, New Delhi, 4 January 2019

CHINA'S 'OWN COURTS' FOR BRI ROWS RAISE EYEBROWS

China's recent announcement that it would establish courts under its own judicial system to handle international disputes arising from projects under the Belt and Road Initiative (BRI) has triggered apprehensions that this would lead to dispute settlement on its unilateral terms and conditions.

Thecourts, which are to be based in Beijing, Xi'an and Shenzhen, have been established under the authority of the Supreme People's Courtof China, ET has learnt.

The Xi'an court will manage commercial disputes for the Silk Road Economic Belt, which connects China, West Asia and Europe. The Shenzhen court will manage commercial cases for the Maritime Silk Road, which connects China, Southeast Asia, Africa and Europe.

Chinese media has reported that the country will seek to promote the courts to resolve disputes that emerge in the BRI. Experts said that the courts could be similar to the International Commercial Court in Singapore and the International Finance Centre Courts in Dubai.

"It is unclear over which authority the Chinese have claimed jurisdiction over BRI disputes," said a note by law firm

Dezan Shira and Associates, which has been guiding foreign investors in India, ASEAN and China since 1992.

"There are existing mechanisms to deal with such matters, ranging from existing bilateral investment treaties to multilateral agreements such as those ASEAN has with China, the 2012 'Agreement on Dispute Settlement Mechanism of the Framework Agreement on Comprehensive Economic Cooperation'," the law firm said.

Most bilateral treaties and the ASEAN treaty provide for similar conflict resolution processes: consultation, followed by mediation, followed by arbitration by an ad-hoc arbitration tribunal, with no preset venue or choice of law, either procedural or substantive, according to the law firm.

The Chinese government is trying to force other sides to accept Chinese mediation and arbitration through its proposal to have these three courts rule on all BRI disputes, experts said.

The country's move to establish BRI-specific courts seems to alter that position, and move jurisdiction specifically to China on bilateral projects.

The memorandum of understanding (MoU) that China has signed with more 70 nations concerning cooperation on BRI projects does not appear to suggest any differing mechanisms for dealing with disputes, other than the usual terminology referring to "friendly consultations," though these may differ from case to case, according to Dezan Shira and Associates.

"The question concerning China's establishment of the BRI courts therefore revolves around the question of how this mechanism was agreed to between China and the BRI nations with which it has signed agreements," it said.

There are other existing alternatives to accepting arbitration in China. These include an agreement reached in September last year between the Singapore International Mediation Centre and the China Chamber of International Commerce Mediation Centre (CCOIC), which entered into an MoU to resolve BRI cross-border disputes.

"Despite these steps by China, the choice of arbitration venue and law, both procedural and substantive, should be left to negotiation between the concerned parties ... third party jurisdictions with established rules and an experienced body of jurists are always preferable to those jurisdictions affiliated with one or the other of the parties to a contract," the law firm said.

The Economic Times, New Delhi, 14 February 2018

Protests in Hambantota against Chinese projects.. *Source:* www.rfa.org.

Protest against Chinese funded infra project. *Source:* The ASEAN Post.

Unutilised Hambantota Port. *Source:* newsin.asia.

III

Debt Trap Looms Large over Parts of South Asia

Chinese Bull in a Lankan Shop

India's southern neighbourhood is in a political flux, crafted by China's ambitions to challenge India's leadership in the region. While the defeat of Maldivian President Abdulla Yameen could not have been better timed for India, former president Mahinda Rajapaksa's re-entry into Sri Lanka's government as PM, through nothing less than a coup of sorts, has brought back memories of when Chinese money made massive inroads during Rajapaksa's presidency.

The Chinese-funded projects in Sri Lanka were later rebranded as being part of the Belt and Road Initiative (BRI). While it pushed the country to a debt trap, China created immense opportunities for Beijing's strategic goals, as the island nation is located in a critical position in the Indian Ocean Region dividing the Arabian Sea and the Bay of Bengal.

While Rajapaksa made a high-profile visit to Delhi a few weeks before his dramatic return to Sri Lankan centre stage attempting to mend fences, his loyalty to China remains firm.

Beijing can indeed take solace from his return at a time when there is pushback against Beijing in Maldives, Malaysia, Myanmar, Bangladesh and even parts of Africa and Europe.

Following the 19th Amendment of the Constitution in 2015, the president can no longer sack the PM at will. The former only has the power to appoint a prime minister if the government loses confidence in Parliament, or if that seat is vacated due to death, resignation or 'otherwise'.

President Maithripala Sirisena's decision to choose the 'otherwise' option stems from his primary aim to join hands with Rajapaksa and spoil exited PM Ranil Wickremesinghe's chances of becoming president in 2020. Sirisena and Rajapaksa have been fellow travellers with the Sri Lanka Freedom Party (SLFP), traditional rivals of Wickremesinghe's United National Party (UNP).

Sri Lanka has a peculiar arrangement, which is neither fully presidential nor fully prime ministerial, but a power-sharing one between president and PM. While the balance of power was earlier in the president's favour, the 19th Amendment significantly brought presidential powers 'under control'.

Though the amendment has given more powers to the Cabinet under the direct purview of the PM, Sri Lanka's defence is under the commander-in-chief of the armed forces—the president. This tips power in favour of the president, especially during an internal political crisis.

While UNP is in dialogue to begin an impeachment process to remove the president, it may not follow things through, as this would require a two thirds majority in Parliament, more than the simple majority that Wickremesinghe needs to 'continue' as PM.

The real test lies ahead when Parliament meets—either over the next few days as desired by UNP, or on 16 November as decided by Sirisena. Dissolving Parliament, however, is beyond Sirisena's purview.

While the marriage between Sirisena and Wickremesinghe was always a matter of convenience, the government safeguarded India's interests with clear message to China that its military mission was unwelcome in Sri Lanka. The two leaders became regular visitors to New Delhi, enabling India to remain regional leader.

The Sri Lankan coalition government, however, could not scrap the Chinese infrastructure projects, since the country owed millions to Beijing. The debts were converted to equities and buybacks by China.

The very presence of Rajapaksa as PM with powers equal to the president—provided Wickremesinghe fails to 'continue/ return'—is advantageous to China. Yet, he can ill afford to alienate India, as his recent Delhi visit proves.

The Economic Times, Op-Ed, 2 November 2018

CHINA MAY PUT SOUTH ASIA ON ROAD TO DEBT TRAP

China's grandiose global connectivity initiative—One Belt One Road (OBOR) or Belt& Road Initiative (linking China with Europe via SE Asia and C Asia through land and sea links)—which is set to receive a formal endorsement at the 14-15 May international meet (OBOR MEET) has the potential of adverse economic implications for countries in South Asia as reflected by the situation in Sri Lankan that has run into a huge debt trap by welcoming Chinese-funded projects.

While the Lankan PM is expected to attend OBOR among 28 other leaders from across the continents, Colombo is running up huge financial losses owing to high interest rates charged by Chinese lenders for the mega infrastructure projects which will now be part of OBOR. Pakistan is no better either as the huge sum of over $50 billion for China-Pakistan-Economic-Corridor can spell doom for an already faltering Pakistani economy.

Debts are turning into equity and finally ownership for Chinese firms that will not only adversely impact Sri Lankan and Pakistani economies but also create security implications for India due to China's constant presence in the periphery. This has major lessons for Bangladesh and Nepal where China has assured to invest billions. While Bangladesh is skipping the OBOR meet, Nepal has downgraded its participation at the meet from the level of President to Deputy PM.

Sri Lanka's growing economic engagement with China has generated concern among scholars and policymakers. China has provided Sri Lanka with over $5 billion between 1971 and 2012, and most of this has gone into infrastructure development, with China investing $1 billion into a deep-water port at Hambantota and billions into the Mattala Airport, a new railway and the Colombo Port City Project.

As a country emerging from civil war, infrastructure is crucial in facilitating Sri Lanka's trade and foreign investment sectors. The World Bank forecasts that Sri Lanka's GDP is likely to grow from 3.9% in 2016 to around 5% in 2017.

Sri Lanka has borrowed billions of dollars from China to build domestic infrastructure. Sri Lanka's estimated national debt is $64.9 billion, of which $8 billion is owed to China—this can be attributed to the high interest rate on Chinese loans. For the Hambantota port project, Sri Lanka borrowed $301 million from China with an interest rate of 6.3%, while the interest rates on soft loans from the World Bank and the Asian Development Bank (ADB) are only 0.25–3%. Interest rates of India's Line of Credit to the neighbouring countries are as low as 1%, or even less, in some cases. Sri Lanka is facing debt crisis or 'debt trap' as some scholars describe it.

Sri Lanka is currently unable to pay off its debt to China because of its slow economic growth. To resolve its debt crisis, the Sri Lankan government has agreed to convert its debt into equity. This may lead to Chinese ownership of the projects finally.

The Lankan decision allowing Chinese firms 80% of the total share and a 99-year lease of Hambantota port caused public outrage and violent protests in Sri Lanka. In addition, Chinese firms have been given operating and managing control of Mattala Airport, built with Chinese loans of $300-400 million, because the Sri Lankan government is unable to bear the annual expenses of $100-200 million. Experts here told ET that such arm twisting of democratic regimes in Lanka to get projects runs contrary to the Chinese position against regime changes in other parts of the world.

Having access to the Hambantota port and Mattala airport provides Beijing with a strategic military position in the event of an Indian Ocean conflict and is also key for its 'Belt and Road' initiative. The growing Chinese influence may also compel Sri Lanka to support China's position on the South China Sea dispute and 'One China' policy.

Pakistan is heading towards a similar crisis if not worse, according to experts who study China-Pakistan-Economic-Corridor closely. China's masterstroke in inducing Pakistan into mortgaging Pakistan's present and future economic prosperity has been achieved by Chinese President Xi Jinping's announcement in 2015 of the much flaunted $46 billion China Pakistan Economic Corridor (CPEC). The Chinese promise for CPEC has now crossed $50 bn and this may turn Pakistan into a client state of Beijing in the real sense of the term, according to a formal official who has served in China and India's neighbourhood in the past.

Projected by China as a Chinese master blueprint for economic transformation of Pakistan, it is a merely a strategic Chinese blueprint for China's colonial control of Pakistan in perpetuity, strategically and economically. Pakistan is being made to take heavy loans from the Chinese banks at high rates of interest to finance the CPEC, and some experts said that Pakistan would take nearly 40 years to pay back these loans. Key voices within Pakistan have been publicly questioning the CPEC's economic benefits to Pakistan, pointing out that the virtual and real economic benefits accrue only to China."

The Economic Times, New Delhi, 2 May 2017

SOUTH ASIAN NATIONS START REVISITING CHINA'S BRI, THE GREAT PUSHBACK BEGINS

China is facing a push back against its BRI in South Asia including from local politicians in Balochistan and this could emerge as a headache ahead of second BRI Summit.

While resistance from Baloch political parties and Balochistan government against BRI is on rise, Maldives is undertaking an internal exercise to ascertain money owed to Beijing under BRI.

India's southern neighbour Sri Lanka, notwithstanding new loans from China, is courting other powers to bring back balance in its foreign policy. Bangladesh, despite growing trade with China, remains sceptical of borrowing $ 25 bn promised by Xi under BRI two years back, according to persons who monitor BRI projects in the region.

The pushback against CPEC – flagship project of BRI—in Pakistan is the most striking. Jam Kamal, the chief minister of Balochistan, has amended laws to freeze the sale of land to Chinese companies in Gwadar, ET has learnt.

Local Baloch leaders are up in arms as the impoverished region will hardly benefit from CPEC projects. "Gwadar is not for sale," Aslam Bhootani, a political leader from the port city, recently told media. Baloch insurgents are on a warpath against CPEC and are targeting Chinese officials.

While Gwadar gives China much coveted access to the Indian Ocean Region, Beijing has failed to take into consideration local sentiments in Balochistan by depending on a friendly government in Islamabad.

In Maldives, the projects under review include a landmark bridge, the expansion of an international hospital, and roads—all funded by China, sources from Male told ET. On 29 January, Maldives' attorney general announced the government was seeking foreign help to examine the records. Maldives ministry of finance has set up its own task force to investigate the contracts signed with China by President Abdullah Yameen.

After Yameen lost polls last September, Chinese Ambassador to Madlives Zhang Lizhong presented former president Mohamed Nasheed, a note stating the Maldives owed China $3.2 billion—more than double the $1.3 billion worth of Chinese loans on official books. Nasheed is a relative and advisor to the current Maldives president. China's foreign ministry dismissed the incident as "false."

In Sri Lanka, which is caught in an external debt crisis, the government is now seeking support from Japan and India. Recently, a US aircraft carrier also received logistics supply from Colombo. The $1.5 billion Hambantota Port on the southern coast is now in Chinese hands after a controversial debt-for-equity swap. Besides China is funding the $1.4 billion port City, a 269-hectare area of land reclaimed from the waters off Colombo.

Chinese infrastructure development loans to Sri Lanka stand at $9.2 billion. Chinese loans for infrastructure projects have come with interest as high as the benchmark London Interbank Offered Rate plus 6%, sources from Colombo told to ET.

Last month, Sri Lanka announced a $1.85 billion light rail system in Colombo, to be built by Japan with concessional loans. Subsequently, India offered a new set of trains to upgrade Sri Lanka's railways through $1.3 billion in concessional financing. In Bangladesh, there is quiet unease over the $24 billion pledged—but not yet disbursed—for BRI. The Hasina government has gone slow with amid resistance from the country's finance ministry.

Of the 115 countries that BRI touches, Asia accounted for 39% of the contract value from January 2014 to June 2018, higher than Africa's 30%, according to Moody's Investors Service. Criticisms are rife that China is seeking not only financial profits but political gains from the BRI.

The Economic Times, New Delhi, 12 February 2019

HERE'S WHY INDIA SKIPPED CHINA'S OBOR SUMMIT

India's decision to skip One Belt One Road (OBOR) or Belt and Road Initiative (BRI) Summit in Beijing between May 14-16 is a strategic call with the mega connectivity initiative in its current form in various parts of South Asia having no less implications than China Pakistan Economic Corridor (CPEC).

OBOR in its current form encompasses all of South Asia sans India and Bhutan and enhances China's strategic heft in the same countries where India also has huge stakes including connectivity initiatives and infrastructure projects launched during past three years.

Beijing, persons familiar with OBOR pointed out, did not take Delhi in confidence when it unilaterally decided to introduce and implement projects in many of the South Asian countries. Such projects in their current form not only have the potential to push the countries into financial crisis having direct bearing on India but also have strategic implications for Delhi during times of conflict, according to one of persons quoted above.

India in keeping with its principle of taking local sentiments on board is in the process of implementing several connectivity initiatives both through bilateral format as well as sub-regional groups—BBIN and BIMSTEC—across the region. These initiatives complement connectivity projects in Southeast Asia under the Modi government's Act East Policy. Simulataneously Chabahar Port and International North South Transportation Corridor are expected to enhance India's footprints in Russia, Central Asia, Iran, Afghanistan and Europe.

In message to China's unilateral approach, MEA Spokesperson Gopal Baglay on Saturday night stated that India is of firm belief that connectivity initiatives must be based on universally recognized international norms, good governance, rule of law, openness, transparency and equality.

CPEC that is being constructed through PoK bypassing repeated Indian protests can impact geo-politics of the region and this explains India's sensitivity with the project. ET has learnt that India been issuing strong demarches to Beijing for over 50 years since 1961 at each and every stage of Chinese engagement with Pak occupied Kashmir.

The first such demarche was issued by Indian Ambassador to China one year before the 1962 Sino-Indian War. Subsequent demarches were issued in 1963, 1965, 1968, 1969, 1982, 1983 and protests were continuously registered since 2008 when China and Pakistan agreed to construct first mega infrastructure project in PoK. Thereafter PM Narendra Modi, Foreign Minister Sushma Swaraj, NSA Ajit Doval and Foreign Secretary S. Jaishankar have raised India's concerns about China-Pakistan-Economic-Corridor with Chinese leadership on numerous occasions since 2014.

The 1961 demarche was the first-time when India protested Beijing's attempt to give recognition to Pakistan's illegal occupation of Kashmir. "In India's view Pakistan has no borders with China; to be frank, India thinks Pakistan and China cannot manage the borders of a third country ... we know about your dispatching sentinels to border areas, but if it goes beyond that, if you state that you are willing to consider negotiating borders with Pakistan, there will be sharp reactions on India's part ... India cannot be blamed for the consequences that occur...." stated the 1961 demarche given by then Indian Envoy to Beijing to Vice Foreign Minister of China Geng Biao and Director Zhang Wennji at that time.

A similar demarche was extended by MEA to the Chinese Embassy in India on 2 March 1963. The demarche expressed India's deep concern over China's "persistence in continuing their arbitrary and illegal efforts to locate and align the boundary between China and the areas of Kashmir which has been illegally occupied by Pakistan." In less than five months another demarche by issued by MEA to the Chinese Embassy in July 1963 which stated that China has neither rights or legality to negotiate with Pakistan on Kashmir. Another demarche was issued in September 1963. It may be recalled that China and Pakistan signed a boundary agreement in 1963 wherein PoK divides the two countries. China has continued to pay only lip service to India's concerns so far.

"Connectivity projects must be pursued in a manner that respects sovereignty and territorial integrity.... The so-called 'China-Pakistan Economic Corridor,' which is being projected as the flagship project of the BRI/OBOR, the international community is well aware of India's position. No country can accept a project that ignores its core concerns on sovereignty and territorial integrity," noted Baglay.

The Economic Times, New Delhi, 15 May 2017

President-elect Ibu Solih may Look at Halting BRI Projects in Maldives

Maldives President-elect Ibu Solih is exploring options of putting on hold Chinese-funded Belt & Road Initiative (BRI) projects that have caused India major concerns about Beijing's increasing influence in the Indian Ocean neighbourhood.

ET has learnt that Solih might follow the example of Malaysian PM Mahathir Mohammad, who has put on hold mega BRI projects in his country after returning to power earlier this year.

There is talk that the new Maldivian President might even cancel some BRI projects that were encouraged by his predecessor and outgoing leader Abdullah Yameen. Yameen allegedly received $1.5 million as poll financing, with his critics accusing him of obtaining the funds from Beijing.

Solih's challenge will, however, be the repayment of Chinese loans extended for the projects in the island-nation. Maldives is facing liabilities of $1.4 billion, accounting for about a third of the country's GDP, due to Yameen's policies. Seventy-five percent of the debt was generated from the BRI projects. During his campaign, Solih spoke against Chinese debt that brought financial difficulties for Maldives.

Former President Md Nasheed—Solih's biggest backer—has declared reviewing all the agreements that Maldives had signed with China under Yameen's five-year rule between 2013 and 2018, hours after his MDP won the Presidential polls on 24 September.

Maldives, a small economy heavily reliant on tourism, is one of the most at-risk countries of any involved with the BRI because of debt, according to the Center for Global Development, a Washington DC-based think-tank tracking the initiative.

In 2014, China began to develop major infrastructure projects in the archipelago. One is a bridge linking the capital Male to a nearby island. The other is an expansion of the capital's airport, a project awarded to a Chinese company in 2014.

The Maldives has also leased an uninhabited island (Feydhoo Finolhu) to a Chinese enterprise for 50 years at a price of around $4 million, with plans to develop infrastructure for tourism. China is also constructing a 25-storey apartment complex and hospital in the Maldives. China and Maldives had signed an FTA in September 2017.

After the shock election result in the Maldives, Beijing has suggested it wants to join hands with India to stabilise the Indian Ocean country.

The Economic Times, New Delhi, 19 October 2018

Rising anti-China protests in Philippines. *Source:* The Diplomat.

Anti-Chinese demonstration in Hanoi.
Source: Southeast Asia Globe.

Protests against China-run copper mine in Myanmar. *Source:* The Irrawaddy.

IV

South East Asia's Belt and Road Conundrum

South East Asian Peers Back India's Stance on Belt and Road Initiative

Key SE Asian nations have echoed India's position on President Xi Jinping's Belt and Road Initiative (BRI) and expresses concerns over the Chinese debt trap ahead of the second BRI summit to be convened by Beijing.

As many as 70 per cent of the entities respondents in a recent survey conducted by a Singapore think tank among Govt and non-Govt stakeholders in Malaysia, Philippines and Thailand pointed out that their governments in order to manage the risk of shouldering high debts, should take a very careful and conservative attitude when discussing BRI.

One third of those surveyed complained about the (lack of) transparency of the One Belt One Road plan, and 16 percent predicted the plan will eventually fail. Around half of the people surveyed recognized that China has a more superior regional influence than the U.S.

As much as 60 per cent of the respondents in the survey expressed the belief that the U.S.' global power has declined in the past year. One third even thought the U.S. has completely lost its influence in the region.

India has not joined BRI and has expressed strong reservations on funding pattern and objectives of the mega plan. Besides, India has made no bones about the fact that big Chinese loans under BRI is pushing countries towards debt trap. Delhi is also hoping to create connectivity projects in SE Asia based on requirements of the countries in the region.

But it is not just SE Asia that is worried with Chinese ambitions. The Federation of German Industries has recently called on the European Union to take a stronger economic position against Mainland China to help EU companies fight against unfair competitive methods like product dumping, compulsive technology transfer, and inequality in financial backing.

The Federation made its official announcement on January 10 with 54 requests for the German government and the EU to provide assistance. The announcement emphasized that, while German companies need the Chinese market, the Chinese government has refused to provide necessary market access.

The Federation has also called for establishing a stronger economic framework to regulate companies from non-market economies. The announcement highlighted the requests to stop subsidizing products not manufactured in the EU and to increase EU investments on EU infrastructure and innovation.

The German Federation is the joint organization of 36 industrial associations. It is the most important lobbying organization representing the German Industries.

The Economic Times, New Delhi, 12 January 2019

CHINA'S OBOR INITIATIVE MAY CREATE POLITICAL AND ECONOMIC INSTABILITY IN SOUTHEAST ASIA; INDIA WARY

India is closely watching China's growing influence over Southeast Asian countries. Although India has undertaken infrastructure and capacity building projects in these countries over the past three years, under the Narendra Modi government's Act East Policy, experts warn that massive Chinese investments under its 'One Belt, One Road' initiative may create political and economic instability in the region, impacting India.

Chinese investments are aimed at not only regional connectivity but also ideological hegemony, with countries such as Cambodia and Laos increasingly getting drawn into its sphere of influence, said one of the experts, who did not wish to be identified.

Cambodia, Laos, Indonesia and Myanmar are planning to attend a meeting on OBOR being convened by China on May 14-15. Certain reports suggest that Vietnam's top leader may, however, skip the meet given the lukewarm political relations between the two countries.

China is constructing the North-South Transport Link from Southern China to the Southeast Asian countries. According to the Asian Development Bank, Southeast Asian countries need huge investments in energy supply, transportation, telecommunication, water capacity and sanitation to keep pace with their economic growth and growing populations.

With infrastructure development, especially railway networks, requiring big-ticket investments, China's economic prowess makes its political ambitions achievable, experts from India and Southeast Asia said.

However, increased economic relations have not yet translated into a deeper security cooperation between China and many Southeast Asian countries. According to many Chinese commentators, these countries will take money but not sign up to the political, cultural and security requirements of

China's vision of a "community of shared destiny." Singapore, Vietnam and Myanmar are a few such examples.

Singapore emphasises on a rules-based global order amid China's claims in South China Sea region. Tensions are high between Myanmar and China over Chinese funded dam and port projects in the country. Vietnam has had lukewarm political ties with China for decades and China's aggressive moves in South China Sea have sharpened the divide. Indonesia and Malaysia are increasingly getting uncomfortable over this as well, notwithstanding the fact that China is undertaking several infrastructure related projects in both these countries.

Experts warn that Cambodia may be heading for a Sri Lankan type debt crisis situation. Cambodia, one of China's closest international partners and diplomatic allies, is truly under China's economic and political influence. Cambodian Prime Minister Hun Sen recently described China as Cambodia's "most trustworthy friend." Similarly, Chinese President Xi Jinping described Cambodian King Norodom Sihamoni Cambodia "like a brother" when he visited Beijing in June 2016.

China is now Cambodia's largest military supplier and provider of development aid and foreign investment, having given nearly $3 billion in loans and grants to the country since 1992. A 2016 International Monetary Fund report showed that Cambodia's external multilateral public debt is now at $1.6 billion, while its bilateral public debt with China is $3.9 billion.

While Cambodia and Sri Lanka are different in terms of their geographic location, demography and nature of strategic relations with China, there are some crucial lessons that Cambodia and other small countries in the region can learn to avoid ending up in Sri Lanka's position. Cambodia needs to diversify its borrowing sources and consider taking loans from multilateral bodies and countries such as India and Japan, experts said. Cambodia will also need to diversify its foreign policy to include other countries and regional initiatives such as ASEAN and Mekong Ganga Cooperation, experts said.

China's influence in Cambodia is growing in tandem with increasing loans. This is evident in Cambodia's decision to ban the Taiwanese flag from being raised in Cambodia. This could be true for other countries in India's periphery as well including Maldives. Maldives has leased an island close to Male airport for 50 years at the cost of $4 billion to a Chinese company, a development that could have adverse strategic implications for India. China has been eyeing opportunities to help build infrastructure in Maldives to expand its footprint in the Indian Ocean Region as part of the One Belt, One Road project.

The Economic Times, New Delhi, 4 May 2017

MYANMAR TO TRIM CHINESE LOANS TO AVOID DEBT TRAP

China's Belt and Road Initiative (BRI) has hit a hurdle in Myanmar—a key pillar in BRI like Pakistan—with the host government reducing the scope of Beijing's loans for Kyaukpyu Port in Rakhine state, fearing a debt trap.

China had planned to fund $7.3 bn for Kyaukpyu Deepwater Port project, but will now be allowed to invest only $1.3 bn for the initiative, ET has learnt. Myanmar's officials indicated to ET that the government wants to avoid debt trap by accepting huge loans from China that comes with high interest rate.

The project's original plan was to construct 10 berths for large oil tankers in the deep-water port, but it has been whittled down to two.

The Chinese foreign ministry though has claimed that the negotiation is still on. The primary developer, China CITIC Group, claims that the $1.3 bn is for the "initial phase," which is one of the four phases.

The Myanmar government has stated that it will not provide sovereign guarantees for any loans to the project and the government will require a third-party independent audit on project spending.

The port of Kyaukpyu (Rakhine state) is located right at the entry point of the China-Myanmar Oil and Gas Pipeline and the key pillar for BRI, liking the Indian Ocean to the southern part of China. In December 2008, China and Myanmar had signed a deal to construct an oil pipeline at Kyaukphyu enabling Beijing to avoid the Malacca Straits for transport of oil sourced from West Asia. India has constructed Sittwe Port also in Rakhine state and the Special Economic Zone (SEZ) is being set up there.

Loans for BRI have raised fears of countries falling into a debt trap as it happened with Sri Lanka and Cambodia.

But it is not just the Myanmar government that had red flagged China's economic strategy, the German government too has issued warnings about China's acquisition efforts and has encouraged European companies to join forces to take on the competition from China.

Leading German media house Deutsche Welle recently reported that China has been obtaining state-of-the-art technology through the acquisition of foreign companies. It has also been acquiring infrastructure projects in Europe in order to gain political influence.

Thomas Bareiß, secretary of the Committee on Economic Affairs and Energy, said that the German government inspected

80 acquisition proposals in 2017 and 30% of such requests were from Chinese companies.

Bareiß said although Germany is a country that is very open to foreign investment, it should not underestimate the acquisition attempts by these Chinese investors and all the Eastern European countries should unite on the issue.

Deutsche Welle quoted him saying, "We can't be too naive and too reckless. The competition in the international community requires a tough position. We are willing to face it, but it must be under fair and equal rules of the game. We are still far from it because the investment environment around the world is very different."

Recently, for the second time, China's state-owned company, the China Grid Corporation of China (SGCC), failed to acquire a 20% stake in the German transmission system operator, 50Hertz.

The Economic Times, New Delhi, 31 August 2018

V

African Dilemma: China a Partner or Neo-Coloniser

China's OBOR Initiative could Worsen Socio-Economic Difficulties for Africa

Africa—undergoing a bitter experience in the aftermath of Chinese investments in the continent—may face more trouble after China's mega One Belt One Road (OBOR) connectivity initiative—that gives Beijing strategic foothold in the region —is rolled out.

Chinese policy to harness raw material and export finished products to African nations have left the locals without fair share of jobs, killed local manufacturing industry, pushed the countries towards debt and created social tensions. It is felt that the mega infra projects under OBOR would exacerbate socio-economic difficulties for African nations, some among the fastest-growing economies in the world.

The precarious situation has encouraged some African nations to move closer to India that share decades old bonds with the continent since the days of anti-colonial struggle. Only two African leaders (Ethiopia and Kenya) are attending 14-15 May OBOR meet organised by China but officials across countries from the continent point out that discomfort with Beijing is on the rise.

Anti-China Protests in Africa. *Source:* Internship China.

Protests by Ethiopians at Chinese Embassy USA. *Source:* Ethiopian Review.

China performs 1st live drills in overseas base in Djibouti.
Source: R.T.com

A senior Chinese official, speaking on the condition of anonymity, noted that India should also send representative to the OBOR meet despite differences on other issues and cited example of Japan, which despite sharper differences with Beijing, is sending an official for 14-15 May forum. China may have built stadiums, airports, hospitals, highways and dams across the continent, but these projects have left many African countries saddled with debts, environmental conflicts and labour strikes, point out the officials quoted above.

"This is nothing but pouring China's overcapacity overseas And OBOR wants to further accentuate the situation—by pouring Chinese steel and concrete onto local ecology at recipient cost. OBOR is mediaeval mercantilism in postmodern times," alleged a scholar who has studied China's foreign policy and forays into Africa for decades.

India's development model is gaining traction in Africa as an alternative to the Chinese model. The mega Indo-African summit in Delhi in 2015 and visits by the president, vice president and PM across Africa in 2016 have raised Delhi's profile in the continent. Africa's interest in what India stands for and offers have been growing, officials here told ET.

In an opinion piece published in the *Financial Times* in 2013, Nigeria's Central Bank governor, Lamido Sanusi, said Chinese investment in sub-Saharan Africa smacked of 'colonialism,' in size and style. Beijing was accused of holding back a growing African economy by focusing on the pursuit of raw materials, rather than on the creation of local markets and jobs.

China has been discomfited on occasions. In 2014, South African President Jacob Zuma cautioned that Africa's somewhat lopsided trade ties with China were turning out to be "unsuitable in the long term." In Zambia, in 2015, the government had to take control of a Chinese copper mine after numerous complaints of labour abuse. That same year, Botswana's President Ian Khama called for a reduction in new contracts to Chinese companies, citing poor construction and delays.

Ghana and Angola too have been unhappy over Chinese products and social tensions due to Chinese approach in ignoring local populace. Attempting to change its image before OBOR Summit, Chinese Foreign Minister Wang Yi made a tour of Africa earlier this year.

India has had centuries-old connections with Africa with brisk travel and trade across the Indian Ocean, colonial linkages and ties forged in the post-colonial days of South-South cooperation and third world solidarity. India has offered developmental assistance and lines of credit to African partners even while undertaking economic reforms at home.

Modi has given a new focus to India's African interaction in his usual energetic style with a more visible engagement. Yet this outreach is benign in nature and in keeping with India's soft power approach to international relations. India's main focus in Africa has been on trade and investment, energy security and developmental assistance; in recent days, maritime security, agriculture and food security have also gained priority.

India is also involved in key capacity building initiatives that include scholarships to hundreds of students from the continent besides hugely successful pan E-Africa project—matched by very few countries even from the developed world. Notably medical tourism to India from Africa is on the rise.

Indian investment in Africa was initiated by government-owned enterprises that have stakes in the mining and energy sector. But it is private sector investment that has fuelled a substantial part of Indian investment as opportunities opened up in the African markets with several high growth economies.

Indian investments in the continent amount to $33 billion. Trade has been on an upward swing and currently at an estimated $70 billion. As Modi imparts greater energy in India's African relationship, India-Africa alliance is certainly likely to grow larger and deeper.

The Economic Times, New Delhi, 6 May 2017

AFRICA CANCELS A BELT AND ROAD INITIATIVE PROJECT FOR THE FIRST TIME

Sierra Leone, one of the world's developing countries, has scrapped plans to build a China-funded $318-million airport outside the capital, Freetown.

This is the first instance of an African country announcing the cancellation of a China One Belt One Road project. The World Bank and the International Monetary Fund (IMF) both warned earlier that this project may bring an unnecessary debt burden to Sierra Leone.

The mega-project, which was due to be completed in 2022, had been commissioned by former Sierra Leone president Ernest Bai Koroma. But the new president, Julius Maada Bio, has since reassessed the huge loans offered by China to his predecessor.

Under former president Koroma, who was in office from September 2007 until April this year, the country took on $224 million of Chinese debt—$161 million of which was borrowed in 2016 alone, according to the Johns Hopkins SAIS China-Africa Research Initiative.

"After serious consideration and diligence, it is the Government's view that (it) is uneconomical to proceed with the construction of the new airport when the existing one is grossly under utilized," said a letter from the country's Minister of Transport and Aviation to the project's director, published in local media.

African countries jointly owe China about $130 billion, according to the China-Africa Research Initiative. This amount has funded transport, power and mining projects in the resource rich continent.

At this year's Forum on China-Africa Cooperation (FOCAC) summit,, Chinese President Xi Jinping announced a further $60 billion in loans and aid for the continent.

"Countries around the world are now rethinking the readily available loans offered by China for infrastructure projects in their countries, after fearing they could fall prey to Beijing's debt-trap diplomacy... China-funded projects also require the hiring of Chinese-owned contractors rather than local companies and workers. Chinese loans, with interest rates of 2-3 per cent, are 1,100 per cent more expensive than those from Japan, at only 0.25-0.75 per cent," reports Philippine Daily Inquirer.

The Economic Times, New Delhi, 25 October 2018

Protests against BRI in Melbourne. *Source:* The Epoch Times.

BRI: String of Pearls. *Source:* Pakistan Today.

Anti-China protests in Philippines. *Source:* ASEAN Economist.

VI

China's Geo-Political Ambitions Face Pushback

PUSHING BACK AGAINST CHINA'S ONE BELT ONE ROAD, INDIA, JAPAN BUILD STRATEGIC 'GREAT WALL'

India and Japan are together embarking upon multiple infrastructure projects across Africa, Iran, Sri Lanka and Southeast Asia in what could be viewed as pushback against China's massive, unilateral infrastructure initiatives under the One Belt One Road (OBOR) project connecting it with Europe and Africa.

India has conspicuously stayed away from the so-called New Silk Road, launched with much fanfare by Chinese President Xi Jinping on Sunday, because of strategic and security concerns.

While in East Africa, Delhi and Tokyo are planning to fund infrastructure and capacity building projects, Japan is expected to join the Indian foray into the expansion of Iran's Chabahar port and the adjoining special economic zone. In eastern Sri Lanka, the two countries are expected to jointly expand the strategically located Trincomalee port. They are also likely to join hands to develop Dawei port along the Thai-Myanmar border.

India and Japan are holding a separate session on 24 May with stakeholders from Africa on the sidelines of the Africa

Development Bank meeting in Ahmedabad to discuss joint projects on capacity building and infrastructure.

Japan's state minister of finance will lead the country's delegation at the meet.

The India-Japanese initiatives are part of the Freedom Corridor that stretches from the Asia-Pacific to Africa.

It is aimed at stabilising the region amid Chinese designs on it that have led to discomfiture in certain capitals, noted an expert on the issue of international connectivity projects.

The corridor was announced by Japanese Prime Minister Shinzo Abe during counterpart Narendra Modi's trip to Tokyo last November for the annual summit of the two nations. The issue of collaborations also figured in discussions that finance minister Arun Jaitley had during his recent trip to Japan.

India and Japan have launched their own infrastructure development projects to balance China's influence in the region. The central features of this are Japan's Partnership for Quality Infrastructure (PQI) besides collaborations in northeast India and the Andaman and Nicobar Islands. PQI is an initiative for advancing Japan's expertise in infrastructure development, especially against the backdrop of increasing competition to build economic corridors. The initiative was launched by Abe in May 2015.

DEEPENING TIES

"India and Japan's deepening economic partnership has been prompted by a recognition of China's efforts to enhance its influence by funding development projects in its neighborhood," Darshana Baruah of Carnegie India wrote in a recent paper. "China plans to build a corridor of infrastructure projects across both land and sea routes connecting Southeast

Asia to Europe.... As China extends its influence and reach throughout Asia, Japan and India naturally are seeking to do the same. The recent upturn in economic engagement between India and Japan is founded on the twin pillars of development assistance and infrastructure development to enhance domestic and regional connectivity."

Both the continental and maritime routes of OBOR are of strategic concern for India and therefore there are security-related reasons for New Delhi to pursue closer cooperation with Tokyo in response to Beijing's expansionary moves.

"Japan's use of official development assistance as a tool of economic statecraft seems to be directed toward reinforcing its dominance as an aid donor while counterbalancing China's expansion," Baruah further explained in her paper entitled Toward Strategic Economic Cooperation between India and Japan.

"China's increasing military and political assertiveness in Japan's immediate security environment is a key driver of this change."

By expanding their bilateral relationship to include joint infrastructure development across Asia and Africa, Abe and Modi are looking to leverage Japan's economic and India's strategic outreach beyond South Asia to the broader Indian-Pacific Ocean region.

"Africa is the next big destination. India-Japan partnership will unlock Africa's true economic potential," said Prabir De, India's foremost connectivity expert and chair of the India-Asean Centre in noted think-tank RIS. "Mekong-India Economic Corridor (MIEC) connecting Kenya-Tanzania-Mozambique (KTM) growth zone through Jawaharlal Nehru and Kochi ports will open up new vistas of Africa-Asia connectivity."

The Economic Times, New Delhi, 16 May 2017

INDIA, JAPAN COME UP WITH AAGC TO COUNTER CHINA'S OBOR

India on Thursday announced a vision document for Asia-Africa Growth Corridor (AAGC) at the ongoing African Development Bank meeting in Gujarat. The initiative, which comes amid China's mega One Belt One Road project to connect Asia with Africa, is a joint vision of Prime Minister Narendra Modi and his Japanese counterpart Shinzo Abe. It aims for Indo-Japanese collaboration to develop quality infrastructure in Africa, complemented by digital connectivity.

The AAGC, based on India's decades old goodwill in Africa and Japan's financial resources, aims to be an efficient and sustainable mechanism for linking economies, industries and institutions, ideas and people among, and between, Africa and Asia in an inclusive fashion.

There is still vast and untapped potential among, and in between, Asia and Africa, which needs to be explored for shared growth, development, peace, prosperity and stability of these regions, officials said. The opportunities and aspirations in the two regions can be connected through the proposed corridor, they said.

"The AAGC would consist of four main components: development and cooperation projects, quality infrastructure and institutional connectivity, capacity and skill enhancement and people-to-people partnerships. These four components are complementary to promote growth and all round development in both the continents," the document said.

The meeting in Gujarat was attended by two presidents and one vice president from Africa.

The AAGC initiative is part of Indo-Pacific freedom corridor being put in place by India and Japan with an eye on counterbalancing China's OBOR.

Digital connectivity will also support the growth of innovative technology and services between Asia and Africa. There is scope for Asia to share its experiences of growth and development with Africa, according to persons involved in the project.

"Quality infrastructure connects people, towns, regions and countries, and helps unleash their potential for growth. It consists of five remarkable aspects. These aspects are: (a) effective mobilisation of financial resources; (b) their alignment with socio-economic development and development strategies of partner countries and regions; (c) application of high-quality standards in terms of compliance with international standards established to mitigate environmental and social impact; (d) provision of quality of infrastructure taking into account aspects of economic efficiency and durability, inclusiveness, safety and disaster-resilience, sustainability as well as convenience and amenities; and (e) contribution to the local society and economy," the document said.

The quality infrastructure as envisaged by the AAGC "would remain in harmony with the local environment, community, and people's livelihoods." China has often been accused, particularly in Africa, of imposing and executing projects ignoring local sentiments.

India has a long history of development cooperation in Africa in capacity building and contributing towards development of social sector through several unique programmes such as Pan Africa e-Network. Indian companies have sustainable presence in the African region. The EXIM Bank is the lead organisation for carrying out the development credit tasks. India has a distinction in providing affordable, appropriate and adaptable technology. It is also working in project execution and in building technical capacities in many developing countries in the region, officials said.

The Economic Times, New Delhi, 26 May 2017

EU ENVOYS SLAM CHINA'S BELT AND ROAD INITIATIVE, SAYS IT WILL HIT FREE TRADE

Ambassadors of 27 of the 28 European Union countries in Beijing have compiled a report slamming China's Belt and Road Initiative (BRI), claiming that it would adversely impact free trade and put Chinese companies at an unfair advantage.

The report, which has come out at a time when Prime Minister Narendra is in Europe, promoting India as a growing partner for the continent, says the BRI "runs counter to the EU agenda for liberalising trade and pushes the balance of power in favour of subsidised Chinese companies."

The report is part of the EU's preparations for an EU-China summit in July. The European Commission is working on a strategy paper to forge a common EU position on BRI, which will run through 65 countries in six economic corridors. In May last year, at the maiden BRI summit in Beijing, the EU had refused to sign BRI trade document with China.

The Ambassador of Hungary, whose government is a beneficiary of BRI, was not party to the EU envoys' report.

EU officials said that while Europe should not refuse to

cooperate with China the continent should state its terms. There has been rising concern in Europe over BRI, in line with India's position on the project.

India recently reiterated its position on BRI and said that the so-called China-Pakistan Economic Corridor violated India's sovereignty and territorial integrity. "No country can accept a project that ignores its core concerns on sovereignty and territorial integrity," an external affairs ministry spokesperson said. "We are of the firm belief that connectivity initiatives must be based on universally recognised international norms, good governance, rule of law, openness, transparency and equality, and must be pursued in a manner that respects sovereignty and territorial integrity."

EU is also not in favour of Chinese firms getting preferential treatment for BRI projects. The project, EU officials said, must take into account interests of all participants.

"China's 'One Belt, One Road' will be the new World Trade Organisation—whether we like it or not," CEO of German conglomerate Siemens, Joe Kaeser, told the World Economic Forum in January.

In their report, the 27 ambassadors wrote that China wanted to shape globalisation to suit its own interests. "At the same time the initiative is pursuing domestic political goals like the reduction of surplus capacity, the creation of new export markets and safeguarding access to raw materials," the report said.

The report warned that European companies might not get good contracts if China was not compelled to the European principles of transparency in public procurement, as well as environmental and social standards.

EU officials said China was trying to divide Europe, akin to its policy in Southeast Asia.

The Economic Times, New Delhi, April 2018

BEIJING'S BRI PUSH WILL INCREASE ANTI-CHINA SENTIMENTS: RUSSIAN MEDIA

Russian media for the first time has pulled up China's One Belt One Road, or BRI, and has claimed that more actively China promotes the "One Belt, One Road" policy and the more money it puts in, the louder anti-China protests will grow.

A recent article in a leading Russian daily newspaper Nezavisimaya Gazeta said many people in Central Asian countries believe that China's "One Belt, One Road" initiative exhibits the intention to "occupy Central Asia."

Nezavisimaya Gazeta quoted a Kazakhstan sociologist saying that in 2007 only 18% of the local people disliked Chinese immigrants, which rose to 33% in 2012. By 2017, as many as 46% of the local people "hate" Chinese immigrants, said Nezavisimaya Gazeta.

The article stated that many people in Central Asian countries believe that China's "One Belt, One Road" initiative exhibits the intention to occupy Central Asia. "People who have this mentality are not only concentrated in Kyrgyzstan and Kazakhstan where there is a strong anti-Chinese sentiment. Within a short 10 years, such an attitude has spread throughout Central Asia. It has expanded to different religions and different ethnic groups," the article said.

The newspaper also claimed that China's implementation of the "Belt and Road" and its local business operations have destroyed the ecological environment of Central Asia and have become a hotbed for corruption. The Chinese are "extremely willing to hand over envelopes filled with money to local officials in order to solve problems, including tax issues," said Nezavisimaya Gazeta.

The article juxtaposes BRI with Russia's Eurasian Economic Community as tools of competing influence by Beijing and Moscow in Central Asia. While Russia supports BRI, it also holds the view that BRI cannot be only connectivity initiative and recently signed Caspian Sea Treaty with some former states of the USSR to promote connectivity and economic activity in Eurasia.

Moscow is also encouraging India to get further active in Central Asia bilaterally as well as through SCO to make the region multi-polar. India is currently negotiating FTA with Eurasian Economic Union. Moscow reckons that India should enhance its presence in the big Eurasian space and that the International North-South Transportation Corridor, or INSTC, could join existing corridors in Eurasia.

Caspian Sea Treaty signed last Sunday by leaders of Russia, Iran, Azerbaijan, Kazakhstan and Turkmenistan have opened up opportunities in the sector of energy and Blue economy for India. Caspian Sea holds at least 20 billion barrels of oil and more than 240 trillion cubic feet of gas and there are feelers to Delhi by Moscow to take advantage following the treaty.

The treaty ends differences over whether the Caspian is a sea or a lake, granting it special legal status and clarifying the maritime boundaries of each surrounding country.

The Economic Times, New Delhi, 16 August 2018

UN WARNS ABOUT FINANCIAL RISKS IN CHINA'S ONE BELT ONE ROAD PROJECT

The United Nations, close on the heels of OBOR Summit between May 14-16, has raised a red flag over economic, financial, social and environmental risks of China's Belt and Road Initiative (BRI) across a number of countries that are part of the mega connectivity project.

A recently concluded UN Economic and Social Commission for Asia and the Pacific Study (UNESCAP) has warned of financial risks in countries in south and central Asia where China's announced investment value under BRI is high compared to the relative size of the economy of the recipient country.

The $15 billion China-Uzbekistan investment deal signed in late 2013 is roughly equivalent to a quarter of Uzbekistan's GDP. Similarly, the $37 billion China-Kazakhstan cooperation agreement signed in late 2014 and early 2015 and the $46 billion China-Pakistan agreement in April 2015 each represent over a fifth of GDP level in Kazakhstan and Pakistan, according to the UN study.

China's commitment to Pakistan has now reached $ 62 billion. Similarly, the $24 billion China-Bangladesh agreement in October 2016 is equivalent to almost 20% of Bangladesh's GDP.

"External account indicators for some of these economies are relatively weak. In Kazakhstan, the current account deficit amounted to about 6% of GDP in 2016, while external debt stood at over 80% of GDP in 2015. In Pakistan, foreign external reserves are rather small at about 4 months of imports in early 2017," said the report.

"Relatively easy access to large foreign loans for infrastructure projects, even if most of them tend to be on a concessional basis, can lead to risks through a slight deterioration in trade balance, undermining macroeconomic and balance of payments stability in small economies with underdeveloped financial markets and less effective debt management," the study said regarding the nature of the Chinese loans.

It is no secret that Sri Lanka has run into a huge debt trap by welcoming Chinese funded projects. Sri Lankan debt exceeds $60 billion, more than 10 percent of that is owed to the Chinese. To resolve its debt crisis, the Sri Lankan government agreed to convert its debt into equity. This may lead to Chinese ownership of the projects finally.

The financing for BRI or OBOR related infrastructure projects will require large scale capital investments. An estimate by the Chinese government suggests total investment by China would amount to about $4 trillion. The McKinsey Global Institute (2016) and the Asian Development Bank (2017) estimated.

The Economic Times, New Delhi, 25 May 2017

MALDIVES WON'T BE USED AS A PLAYTHING FOR POWERS IN INDIAN OCEAN: IBRAHIM MOHAMED SOLIH

After Ibrahim Mohamed Solih defeated pro-China Abdullah Yameen in the presidential elections in the Maldives last September, he chose India for his maiden state visit last month. In his first interview as President, Solih told Dipanjan Roy Chaudhury in an email interaction said that the island nation would not allow any anti-India activities from its soil and exhorted that Male would play the role of a stabiliser in the Indian Ocean Region. Excerpts.

Indo-Maldives ties have been lukewarm over the last few years. What are your plans to revive warmth in partnership?

We enjoy centuries of historical and cultural ties with India, and it is unfortunate that over the last few years this traditional relationship was subjected to needless tension. I am very pleased that I was able to visit India for my first state visit and having Prime Minister Modi attend our inauguration was a tremendous honour and a very important symbol of the renewed strengthening of Indo—Maldives ties. We will continue to engage and strengthen our relations with India in the areas of health, culture, tourism and India ocean security and stability.

How do you plan to address India's concern with role of third countries in Maldives particularly in infrastructure sector that could be used for military purposes?

Maldives is a sovereign state and we are very mindful of our geostrategic position in the India Ocean. We are also extremely aware of the need to maintain peace and security in the Indian Ocean especially at a time of increased trade, shipping and geopolitical tensions. We recognise that we have shared security interests with India, and will not be allow our territory—as India will not allow hers—to be used for any activity that is detrimental to the other.

What are your government's expectations from India?

We are very thankful to India for understanding the precarious financial situation we're currently facing, and responding so promptly with a considerable package of budgetary support, financial investment and capacity building. My Government's expectations from India is that we will always enjoy a close and neighbourly relationship bound through historical and cultural ties and a respect for each other's sovereignty while maintaining a safe and secure India ocean region.

How can India and Maldives strengthen their defence and strategic partnership?

India and Maldives have always maintained a strong defence and strategic partnership. We conduct regular naval exercises, coordinated patrolling and maritime surveillance and have an understanding of common priorities such as counter terrorism. I believe greater engagement in these areas including an increase in training opportunities with result in a stronger partnership.

What are your thoughts on Belt and Road Initiative in the backdrop of debt that Maldives incurred under the previous Government?

Our Government is still reviewing the extent of the debt incurred under the previous Government. No doubt, the debt situation has put us in an extremely challenging situation. A vast number of infrastructural projects have been undertaken and we are in the process of reviewing the terms of these agreements.

What role to do you envisage for Maldives in the Indian Ocean Region?

Maldives will not be resigned to a play thing between the great power interests of the Indian Ocean region. As a sovereign state in the middle of the India Ocean, it is our interest to ensure a safe and secure Indian Ocean and we will work with all like-minded partners to do so.

How do you want to restore democracy in Maldives?

I am honoured and humbled by the confidence the Maldivian people have placed in me and our coalition Government. We are fortunate to have won a very challenging election with 58% of the vote. Maldives' journey with democracy has taken quite a few twists and turns. The previous administration's policies risked a complete reversal of the human rights and democratic values that we fought so hard to establish with the 2008 constitution. However, the election has proved that the Maldivian people were not willing to give up on those values and voted in favour of re-establishing the rule of law. I hope to live up to the hopes of the Maldivian people by fulfilling the pledges we advocated for in our manifesto—zero tolerance on corruption, judicial reform, investigations into abuses of power, disappearances and suspicious deaths. We also have an ambitious development program which incorporates the island nature of the Maldives and the pledges decentralised governance, based on greater public consultation.

How do you want to strengthen Maldives institutions to strengthen democracy?

Our manifesto outlined a program of judicial and legislative reform which includes conducting legislative audits to determine the laws and regulations which are lacking and/or are not in line with the constitutional guarantees of human rights and fundamental freedoms. My Government will be transparent, consultative and employ a zero tolerance policy on corruption. Our pledges include the establishment of portals— both online and conventional—to encourage public feedback on Government programs and services, and we have already reversed legislation criminalising defamation.

The Economic Times, New Delhi, 12 January 2019

BANGLADESH AVOIDS CHINESE DEBT TRAP, BUILDING BIGGEST BRIDGE WITH OWN FUNDS

Bangladesh, one of India's closest allies in the neighbourhood, has smartly avoided falling into the Chinese debt trap. Drawing lessons from experiences of Nepal, Sri Lanka and Maldives, it has decided to construct its biggest infrastructure project from its own finances.

Seen as a major achievement of Prime Minister Sheikh Hasina as she seeks re-election, the 20-kilometre-long rail and road bridges over Padma river are being built by self-generated funds to the tune of about Rs. 30,000 crore in local currency. The bridges, along with connecting highways over what is often described as one of the world's most treacherous rivers, are expected to be completed in the next few years.

"There is no international funding for this project and budget has been generated from Bangladesh's own budget to avoid any repayment or debt trap," said a person aware of the matter.

The railroad bridge over Padma river which the World Bank had earlier refused to fund will be part of the Asian Highway connecting Bangladesh with India and Southeast Asia, and generate trade and investments. "It is Hasina's dream project and will be a major non-BRI (China's Belt and Road Initiative) connectivity link in South Asia," the person said, adding the World Bank had earlier refused to fund project on charges of corruption which were baseless. Subsequently Hasina decided to go ahead to generate own resources to fund the mega initiative.

Bangladesh government officials told ET that the bridge would establish a strategic link through capital Dhaka between economically backward southwest Bangladesh and the rest of the country, which is witnessing an economic boom following a decade of stability. The Asian Highway Priority Route No. 1 and Trans Asian Railway will be built through the bridges over Padma river, they said.

One of the officials, who spoke on condition of anonymity, said that Bangladesh's gross domestic product (GDP) would increase 1.26 per cent and regional GDP of southwest Bangladesh would increase 2.3 per cent from the expected spurt in trade and investments. Around 67 per cent of the project has been concluded as of last month when Hasina reviewed the venture.

While some Chinese firms are involved in the execution of the project selected through tenders, the initiative has no exposure to Chinese funds. Bangladesh has been cautious in accepting loans from China and has on occasions rejected Chinese firms vying for infrastructure projects and even blacklisted Chinese firms.

"Bangladesh is uniquely positioned to take advantage of its location in the eastern region of South Asia and the Padma bridge project will play a key role in that endeavour," said an expert on regional connectivity, who did not wish to be identified. "The country will be a centre point of different initiatives that seek to connect Bhutan, India and Nepal with the ASEAN and other East Asian countries."

The expert said that with deeper trade, investment and connectivity linkages within the sub-region, Bangladesh can benefit from new markets, new import sources of high quality and better priced products, and increasing opportunities for transport and logistics services.

The erstwhile Khaleda Zia regime in Bangladesh had strong reservations against granting connectivity and transit to the neighbouring countries on the pretext that it would infringe on the sovereignty of Bangladesh. The Sheikh Hasina-led government, however, realised that granting connectivity and transit was a win-win situation for Bangladesh. India's grant of fresh $2 billion for infrastructure development will also contribute to building corridors for sub-regional connectivity.

The Economic Times, New Delhi, 7 November 2018

EUROPE, JAPAN, US, UAE PREFER INDIA FOR JOINT INFRASTRUCTURE PROJECTS IN AFRICA

India has edged out China as the preferred partner for key European nations, Japan and the United Arab Emirates for joint infrastructure and capacity building projects in Africa.

The UAE, France, Germany, UK and Italy are in talks with India to launch joint projects in Africa owing to India's goodwill created by funding demand driven projects and providing concessional loans for various sectors, according to people aware of the matter.

On the other hand, they said, China's Belt and Road Initiative (BRI) is facing a pushback in Africa, with some countries cancelling or going slow on projects owing to huge debts.

Japan, during Prime Minister Narendra Modi's recent visit to Tokyo, announced a mega health project in Kenya that will be implemented jointly by India and Japan as part of third-country initiatives.

ET has learnt that the UAE could partner India for projects in parts of Eastern Africa where the UAE has strong political connections. "France, Germany, UK and Italy have expressed interest in partnering India in third-country projects in Africa. These countries are expected to outline specific projects where they are interested to partner India," said one of the persons, who spoke on condition of anonymity.

In contrast, Sierra Leone in West Africa recently scrapped plans to build a China-funded $318-million airport outside the capital, Freetown. A few other countries in western and southern Africa have also expressed concern that China's funding pattern could push them into debt trap.

African countries jointly owe China about $130 billion, according to the China-Africa Research Initiative. This amount has funded transport, power and mining projects in the resource-rich continent. "Countries around the world are now rethinking the readily available loans offered by China for infrastructure projects in their countries, after fearing they could fall prey to Beijing's debt-trap diplomacy.... China-funded projects also require the hiring of Chinese-owned contractors rather than local companies and workers. Chinese loans, with interest rates of 2-3 per cent, are 1,100 per cent more expensive than those from Japan, at only 0.25-0.75 per cent," the Daily Inquirer, a leading Philippine English newspaper, recently reported.

The Indian model is benign and completely driven by demands and requirements of the Line of Credit (LoC) recipient countries. India's LoC offered at a concessional rate currently amounts to $25 billion for 263 projects in 62 countries including in Africa. This is besides the grants offered by India.

"Since 2014 the government has emphasised on timely completion of all LoC funded projects by removing dubious companies who were earlier executing the projects particularly in Africa. This has also ended pilferage of funds," an official familiar with the projects under the external affairs ministry's Development Partnership Administration told ET.

"Top Indian corporate firms are now involved in execution of projects. The PM as well as the foreign minister have been reviewing status of projects to ensure timely implementation," he said.

After having expanded sectors for which it offers LoC, India has sought blueprints of specific projects in Africa from the partner countries in Europe. The new sectors include infrastructure projects such as convention centres, which were once China's forte, renewable energy initiatives and defence.

India is on course to implementing a $10 billion LoC announced by the PM at the mega Indo-Africa Summit in 2015, the official cited earlier said, adding that the International Solar Alliance (ISA) has been another instrument to bring India and Africa closer to each other. France is partnering India in ISA. Besides, tele-medicine and tele-education projects are being implemented on a pan-Africa basis.

The Economic Times, New Delhi, 24 November 2018

EU Welcomes Indian Participation for Its Proposed Connectivity Projects Worth 60 bn Euros

The European Union will welcome India's participation in starting joint connectivity projects, including in third countries, under its proposed 60 bn Euro plan that aims to provide options beyond China's Belt and Road Initiative.

"The EU is working on a proposal worth 60 billion euros for seven years for connectivity initiatives and would welcome suggestions from India to join this initiative," EU ambassador to India Tomasz Kozlowski told ET following the launch of a strategy paper for India that emphasises on economically sustainable connectivity projects.

In an oblique critique of the BRI, the EU strategy paper refers to global connectivity projects. The EU and India share the view that the approach to connectivity should be environmentally, economically, socially and fiscally sustainable and provide a level playing field for businesses, while respecting international standards and enhancing governance. The paper is expected to suggest echoing India's stand on the issue.

The EU, according to the paper, should seek opportunities in cooperation with India and other Asian partners to support cooperative and inclusive regional orders and integration, with a rules-based approach. This should include the South Asian Association for Regional Cooperation, the Bay of Bengal Initiative for Multi-Sectoral Technical and Economic Cooperation, ASEAN and the Indian Ocean Rim Association. Cooperation should be expanded with India on the promotion of common principles, including in the Asia-Europe Meeting (ASEM), such as on connectivity.

According to Kozlowski, the EU is ready to assist India with its connectivity projects in third countries. Some European companies are helping India in the strategic Chabahar port project in southeast Iran, the gateway to Afghanistan, Central Asia and beyond, according to the EU envoy.

Kozlowski said the EU proposes to start a dialogue with India on partnership in African countries that would focus on projects based on local requirements and demands. Separately, Italy, France and the UK have shown interest in launching third-country projects in Africa in partnership with India on a bilateral basis.

China's BRI is facing a pushback in Africa, with some countries cancelling or going slow on projects due to the high levels of debt involved. Sierra Leone in West Africa recently scrapped a plan to build a China-funded $318 million airport outside the capital, Freetown. Ghana has cut its exposure to Chinese loans. Other countries in Western and Southern Africa have expressed concern that China's funding pattern is pushing them towards a debt trap. African countries jointly owe China about $130 billion, according to the China-Africa Research Initiative.

The Economic Times, New Delhi, 19 December 2018

INDIA, JAPAN TO DEVELOP PORTS TO COUNTER CHINA

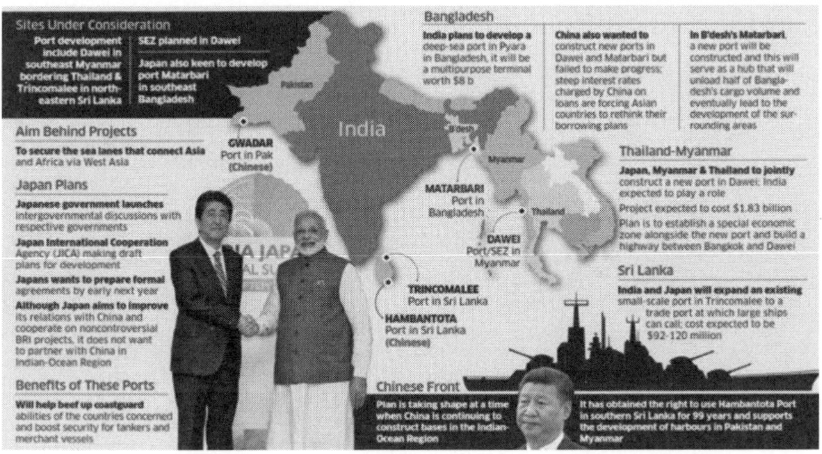

The Economic Times, New Delhi, 30 May 2018